Factoring Nun

Directions: Write the factors for each number as shown in the example:

32 = __1, 2, 4, 8, 16, 32__

28 = _____

9 = _____

4 = _____

33 = _____

6 = _____

7 = _____

Factoring Numbers

Directions: Write the factors for each number as shown in the example:

$$32 = \underline{\hspace{0.3cm} 1, 2, 4, 8, 16, 32 \hspace{0.3cm}}$$

5 = _____

17 = _____

12 = _____

26 = _____

19 = _____

46 = _____

Factoring Numbers

Directions: Write the factors for each number as shown in the example:

$$32 = \underline{1, \, 2, \, 4, \, 8, \, 16, \, 32}$$

$$34 = \underline{\hspace{6cm}}$$

$$5 = \underline{\hspace{6cm}}$$

$$6 = \underline{\hspace{6cm}}$$

$$8 = \underline{\hspace{6cm}}$$

$$4 = \underline{\hspace{6cm}}$$

$$25 = \underline{\hspace{6cm}}$$

Factoring Numbers

Directions: Write the factors for each number as shown in the example:

32 = _1, 2, 4, 8, 16, 32_

10 = _____

39 = _____

19 = _____

48 = _____

1 = _____

7 = _____

Factoring Numbers

32 = ___1, 2, 4, 8, 16, 32___

22 = _____

40 = _____

5 = _____

36 = _____

28 = _____

9 = _____

Factoring Numbers

Directions: Write the factors for each number as shown in the example:

$$32 = \underline{\text{1, 2, 4, 8, 16, 32}}$$

41 = _____

24 = _____

6 = _____

8 = _____

45 = _____

20 = _____

Factoring Numbers

32 = __1, 2, 4, 8, 16, 32__

5 = _____

12 = _____

29 = _____

8 = _____

7 = _____

20 = _____

Factoring Numbers

Directions: Write the factors for each number as shown in the example:

32 =   1, 2, 4, 8, 16, 32

10 = _____

9 = _____

6 = _____

15 = _____

24 = _____

38 = _____

Factoring Numbers

Directions: Write the factors for each number as shown in the example:

$32 =$ ___1, 2, 4, 8, 16, 32___

$28 =$ _____

$50 =$ _____

$22 =$ _____

$6 =$ _____

$13 =$ _____

$25 =$ _____

Factoring Numbers

Directions: Write the factors for each number as shown in the example:

$$32 = \underline{\quad 1, 2, 4, 8, 16, 32 \quad}$$

37 = _____

9 = _____

42 = _____

16 = _____

18 = _____

28 = _____

Exponents

Directions: Solve the following exponents.

$0^{-7} =$ _____

$3^{-7} =$ _____

$1^{-8} =$ _____

$1^{-4} =$ _____

$2^{-2} =$ _____

$3^{0} =$ _____

$6^{-9} =$ _____

$10^{-7} =$ _____

$5^{0} =$ _____

$2^{-9} =$ _____

$0^{-2} =$ _____

$9^{-10} =$ _____

$8^{-5} =$ _____

$8^{-2} =$ _____

Exponents

Directions: Solve the following exponents.

$4^0 =$ _____

$0^{-2} =$ _____

$4^{-8} =$ _____

$9^{-2} =$ _____

$1^{-6} =$ _____

$5^{-4} =$ _____

$6^{-8} =$ _____

$10^0 =$ _____

$10^{-3} =$ _____

$4^{-6} =$ _____

$10^{-8} =$ _____

$2^{-7} =$ _____

$7^{-9} =$ _____

$4^{-2} =$ _____

Exponents

Directions: Solve the following exponents.

6^{-10} = _____

1^{-6} = _____

1^{-4} = _____

0^{-10} = _____

4^{-10} = _____

10^{-3} = _____

3^{-5} = _____

10^{-7} = _____

0^{-3} = _____

3^{-2} = _____

5^{-2} = _____

7^{0} = _____

9^{0} = _____

5^{-8} = _____

Exponents

Directions: Solve the following exponents.

$4^{-7} =$ _____

$4^{-5} =$ _____

$3^{-8} =$ _____

$10^{0} =$ _____

$4^{-6} =$ _____

$5^{-4} =$ _____

$0^{0} =$ _____

$0^{-2} =$ _____

$2^{-7} =$ _____

$3^{-2} =$ _____

$6^{-5} =$ _____

$8^{-7} =$ _____

$10^{-4} =$ _____

$6^{-10} =$ _____

Exponents

Directions: Solve the following exponents.

$7^{-3} =$ _____ $2^{-8} =$ _____

$1^{-4} =$ _____ $6^{-3} =$ _____

$0^{-7} =$ _____ $0^{-4} =$ _____

$9^{0} =$ _____ $9^{-5} =$ _____

$10^{-5} =$ _____ $8^{-9} =$ _____

$1^{-3} =$ _____ $2^{0} =$ _____

$10^{-3} =$ _____ $4^{-6} =$ _____

Add & Subtract & Multiply

Directions: Find the answer.

$28 + 40 + (23 + 24) + 4 \times 3 =$

_____

$14 + (5 \times 5 \times 6 \times 5) \times 3 =$

_____

$24 + 6 + (33 \times 1 \times 5 - 9) =$

_____

$5 \times 7 \times (3 + 26 \times 10) + 29 =$

_____

$5 \times 10 \times 8 + 22 \times (5 \times 1) =$

_____

$1 \times (4 \times 4) \times 9 - 38 + 3 =$

_____

$1 \times (10 + 12 \times 6 + 1) - 23 =$

_____

Add & Subtract & Multiply

Directions: Find the answer.

$5 \times (3 + 11 \times 4 - 18) + 35 =$

_____

$(22 + 33 + 2) \times 8 + 13 - 19 =$

_____

$(10 \times 9 - 17) + 23 \times 2 \times 4 =$

_____

$6 + (22 \times 4) \times 2 - 34 - 40 =$

_____

$30 + (3 - 1 \times 2 + 9) + 22 =$

_____

$6 \times 6 \times 2 + 39 \times (10 - 8) =$

_____

$9 \times 7 - 2 + 37 \times (9 - 5) =$

_____

Add & Subtract & Multiply

Directions: Find the answer.

$(5 \times 4 + 39 + 7) \times 8 \times 6 =$

_____

$7 + (5 + 12 \times 6 \times 7) + 1 =$

_____

$1 \times 2 + 34 + 23 \times (8 + 12) =$

_____

$16 + (8 + 37) + 18 \times 3 \times 4 =$

_____

$(8 \times 9 \times 1 + 37) - 27 + 21 =$

_____

$31 - 15 + 39 + (16 \times 10) \times 3 =$

_____

$40 + (9 \times 3 \times 1) + 9 - 27 =$

_____

Add & Subtract & Multiply

Directions: Find the answer.

(10 + 40) + 19 + 1 - 8 + 33 =

_____

2 × 3 × 3 + (24 - 21 + 23) =

_____

1 × (10 + 37) × 1 × 6 + 23 =

_____

(31 + 30 + 21) + 24 + 20 - 3 =

_____

13 + 23 × 10 + 22 + (22 + 39) =

_____

29 + 15 × (6 + 36 - 33) × 7 =

_____

(21 + 19 + 27 × 4) × 3 - 29 =

_____

Add & Subtract & Multiply

Directions: Find the answer.

$36 + 34 + (1 \times 7 + 14) - 12 =$

_____

$4 + 40 + (17 + 16 - 32) + 26 =$

_____

$11 + 10 + 25 + (33 + 40) + 36 =$

_____

$3 + 27 + 38 + (8 + 3 + 12) =$

_____

$29 - (1 + 12) + 32 + 18 \times 1 =$

_____

$1 \times 4 + 35 + 7 + (20 + 19) =$

_____

$(39 + 22 - 16) + 22 \times 5 + 30 =$

_____

Name: _____   Date: _____

Add & Subtract & Multiply

Directions: Find the answer.

$10 \times 5 - 3 + 31 \times (9 - 9) =$

_____

$5 \times 4 - 17 + 39 \times (10 \times 8) =$

_____

$36 + 5 \times 7 \times (6 \times 5) + 19 =$

_____

$25 - 9 + 17 + (10 + 23 \times 2) =$

_____

$(20 - 6 + 2 \times 7) \times 8 + 3 =$

_____

$5 \times 10 - 13 + 14 + (25 \times 1) =$

_____

$39 + (19 + 28 + 11) + 34 - 12 =$

_____

Add & Subtract & Multiply

Directions: Find the answer.

$8 + (18 \times 3 + 32 - 3) - 12 =$

_____

$(3 \times 3) \times 1 \times 7 - 24 + 36 =$

_____

$6 \times 7 + (24 - 2) + 21 + 15 =$

_____

$6 \times 4 \times (6 + 35 - 28 + 34) =$

_____

$17 + 13 - (5 + 2 \times 6) \times 1 =$

_____

$17 + 11 + (31 \times 2 + 39 - 1) =$

_____

$10 \times 6 \times 9 + 40 - (17 \times 4) =$

_____

Add & Subtract & Multiply

Directions: Find the answer.

$7 \times 9 \times (1 + 5) \times 10 \times 7 =$

_____

$7 \times 2 + 15 \times 7 \times (10 + 6) =$

_____

$28 - 14 + 33 + (28 - 24) \times 3 =$

_____

$39 - 18 + (31 \times 8 \times 10) + 23 =$

_____

$(4 \times 9 + 11 \times 4 - 17) - 20 =$

_____

$9 \times 4 + (1 \times 2 + 19) + 14 =$

_____

$39 + 14 \times 9 \times (9 \times 8 + 13) =$

_____

Add & Subtract & Multiply

Directions: Find the answer.

$(6 \times 6) \times 10 - 40 \times 5 + 36 =$

_____

$8 \times 2 + 30 + 38 + (29 \times 4) =$

_____

$28 + (23 \times 6 - 26 - 36) - 25 =$

_____

$10 \times 9 + 31 - (31 + 2) + 27 =$

_____

$3 \times (8 \times 1 \times 10) + 31 \times 8 =$

_____

$6 \times 4 \times (8 + 28 \times 2) \times 7 =$

_____

$(5 \times 9 \times 5 + 37) + 29 \times 2 =$

_____

Add & Subtract & Multiply

Directions: Find the answer.

$6 \times (2 \times 10 \times 8 + 11 - 13) =$

_____

$6 \times 6 + (9 + 23) \times 1 + 21 =$

_____

$7 \times 4 \times 3 + (30 - 7) + 10 =$

_____

$17 + 10 + 34 - 2 \times (4 \times 4) =$

_____

$10 \times 8 \times 1 \times 4 - (37 + 7) =$

_____

$8 + 2 \times (2 \times 6 \times 10) - 33 =$

_____

$21 + 36 \times (7 + 32 + 5) + 30 =$

_____

Subtraction of Integers

Directions: Find the difference.

(-1) – (-5) = _____   5 – (-4) = _____

(-5) – 1 = _____   (-6) – 4 = _____

(-2) – 3 = _____   6 – (-1) = _____

1 – (-7) = _____   (-7) – (-1) = _____

1 – 2 = _____   (-6) – (-3) = _____

(-10) – (-2) = _____   6 – 10 = _____

(-3) – (-8) = _____   (-9) – 3 = _____

Subtraction of Integers

Directions: Find the difference.

(-5) - (-8) = ____

9 - 7 = ____

(-8) - 10 = ____

(-7) - 3 = ____

(-7) - 6 = ____

(-5) - (-10) = ____

9 - (-3) = ____

8 - (-7) = ____

(-6) - 7 = ____

(-8) - 3 = ____

(-5) - 5 = ____

3 - 4 = ____

(-2) - 6 = ____

(-1) - (-4) = ____

Subtraction of Integers

Directions: Find the difference.

$(-9) - (-3) =$ _____ $(-8) - (-2) =$ _____

$(-1) - 9 =$ _____ $(-2) - (-6) =$ _____

$(-8) - 8 =$ _____ $4 - (-5) =$ _____

$(-1) - 2 =$ _____ $9 - (-8) =$ _____

$9 - (-3) =$ _____ $(-8) - (-6) =$ _____

$4 - (-3) =$ _____ $(-2) - (-8) =$ _____

$(-9) - (-10) =$ _____ $2 - 9 =$ _____

Subtraction of Integers

Directions: Find the difference.

(-3) - (-1) = _____

4 - 7 = _____

1 - (-10) = _____

6 - (-5) = _____

8 - (-6) = _____

(-5) - (-9) = _____

7 - (-6) = _____

(-10) - 2 = _____

(-4) - (-6) = _____

4 - (-2) = _____

8 - (-9) = _____

(-4) - (-5) = _____

(-8) - (-10) = _____

(-8) - 8 = _____

Name:_____ Date: _____

Subtraction of Integers

Directions: Find the difference.

(-6) – 6 = _____   (-8) – 4 = _____

(-7) – (-1) = _____   8 – (-2) = _____

2 – (-7) = _____   1 – 6 = _____

4 – 7 = _____   (-1) – (-3) = _____

3 – (-6) = _____   7 – (-8) = _____

(-5) – (-1) = _____   (-2) – 3 = _____

8 – (-3) = _____   (-7) – 8 = _____

Multiplication of Integers

Directions: Find the answer.

$8 \times (-50) =$ _____

$(-2) \times 60 =$ _____

$(-3) \times (-30) =$ _____

$(-5) \times (-30) =$ _____

$8 \times (-30) =$ _____

$(-2) \times (-30) =$ _____

$(-5) \times 70 =$ _____

$7 \times (-30) =$ _____

$(-1) \times 50 =$ _____

$(-3) \times 70 =$ _____

$(-4) \times (-40) =$ _____

$(-8) \times 40 =$ _____

$1 \times (-30) =$ _____

$(-5) \times (-20) =$ _____

Multiplication of Integers

Directions: Find the answer.

(-7) × 90 = _____

(-8) × 70 = _____

4 × (-50) = _____

(-5) × 20 = _____

2 × (-10) = _____

(-4) × (-90) = _____

(-8) × (-30) = _____

(-9) × 70 = _____

5 × (-30) = _____

(-9) × (-20) = _____

(-1) × (-30) = _____

(-1) × 20 = _____

(-6) × 40 = _____

(-9) × 70 = _____

Multiplication of Integers

Directions: Find the answer.

$(-2) \times 70 =$ _____

$(-4) \times 90 =$ _____

$(-10) \times (-80) =$ _____

$(-8) \times 80 =$ _____

$(-1) \times (-60) =$ _____

$2 \times (-20) =$ _____

$4 \times (-70) =$ _____

$(-1) \times 70 =$ _____

$(-4) \times (-60) =$ _____

$(-6) \times 90 =$ _____

$(-5) \times (-40) =$ _____

$(-8) \times (-10) =$ _____

$(-2) \times (-60) =$ _____

$(-9) \times 40 =$ _____

Multiplication of Integers

Directions: Find the answer.

$(-5) \times 10 =$ _____

$5 \times (-40) =$ _____

$4 \times (-40) =$ _____

$(-8) \times 80 =$ _____

$1 \times (-90) =$ _____

$8 \times (-60) =$ _____

$(-6) \times 50 =$ _____

$(-9) \times 20 =$ _____

$9 \times (-50) =$ _____

$7 \times (-70) =$ _____

$(-2) \times 70 =$ _____

$8 \times (-20) =$ _____

$6 \times (-40) =$ _____

$(-3) \times (-10) =$ _____

Multiplication of Integers

Directions: Find the answer.

$(-4) \times (-20) =$ _____

$2 \times (-60) =$ _____

$6 \times (-90) =$ _____

$8 \times (-70) =$ _____

$(-2) \times 50 =$ _____

$(-10) \times 40 =$ _____

$5 \times (-30) =$ _____

$5 \times (-50) =$ _____

$(-2) \times 20 =$ _____

$4 \times (-30) =$ _____

$(-6) \times 50 =$ _____

$(-5) \times 30 =$ _____

$4 \times (-50) =$ _____

$(-3) \times (-20) =$ _____

Decimals to Mixed Numbers

Directions: Convert to fractions and simplify if possible.

62.8 = _____

57.02 = _____

53.5 = _____

76.88 = _____

67.44 = _____

31.68 = _____

88.8 = _____

34.52 = _____

51.58 = _____

85.4 = _____

40.1 = _____

67.32 = _____

88.7 = _____

22.5 = _____

Decimals to Mixed Numbers

Directions: Convert to fractions and simplify if possible.

49.8 = _____

42.36 = _____

5.8 = _____

46.24 = _____

83.5 = _____

47.6 = _____

80.44 = _____

95.9 = _____

64.5 = _____

70.26 = _____

40.46 = _____

43.64 = _____

44.3 = _____

15.74 = _____

Decimals to Mixed Numbers

Directions: Convert to fractions and simplify if possible.

60.48 = _____

5.12 = _____

59.4 = _____

5.82 = _____

85.92 = _____

33.8 = _____

8.5 = _____

79.08 = _____

28.8 = _____

52.5 = _____

92.22 = _____

25.2 = _____

26.2 = _____

85.12 = _____

Decimals to Mixed Numbers

Directions: Convert to fractions and simplify if possible.

84.46 = _____

86.3 = _____

26.6 = _____

57.5 = _____

72.5 = _____

5.12 = _____

40.2 = _____

51.14 = _____

65.72 = _____

37.22 = _____

20.5 = _____

89.34 = _____

76.5 = _____

47.8 = _____

Decimals to Mixed Numbers

Directions: Convert to fractions and simplify if possible.

3.4 = _____

52.4 = _____

70.84 = _____

66.64 = _____

55.6 = _____

96.24 = _____

16.4 = _____

23.89 = _____

8.5 = _____

62.82 = _____

51.73 = _____

43.6 = _____

14.5 = _____

46.5 = _____

Addition of Integers

Directions: Find the sum.

$(-8) + 2 =$ _____ $(-4) + 3 =$ _____

$(-4) + (-1) =$ _____ $(-6) + (-6) =$ ____

$5 + (-7) =$ _____ $(-8) + (-4) =$ ____

$9 + (-6) =$ _____ $(-7) + 8 =$ _____

$0 + (-4) =$ _____ $(-9) + (-9) =$ ____

$(-3) + 3 =$ _____ $10 + (-7) =$ _____

$(-10) + 8 =$ _____ $7 + (-10) =$ _____

Addition of Integers

Directions: Find the sum.

2 + (-4) = _____

4 + (-5) = _____

0 + (-3) = _____

7 + (-5) = _____

(-2) + (-6) = _____

(-6) + (-6) = _____

(-8) + 2 = _____

(-4) + (-6) = _____

7 + (-1) = _____

(-5) + 5 = _____

6 + (-8) = _____

(-8) + 7 = _____

(-9) + 7 = _____

1 + (-8) = _____

Addition of Integers

Directions: Find the sum.

6 + (-6) = _____   6 + (-5) = _____

9 + (-10) = _____   6 + (-4) = _____

(-2) + 4 = _____   (-4) + (-2) = _____

1 + (-2) = _____   2 + (-5) = _____

(-6) + (-2) = _____   (-4) + (-10) = _____

(-9) + 3 = _____   (-1) + (-4) = _____

(-5) + 3 = _____   8 + (-2) = _____

Addition of Integers

Directions: Find the sum.

2 + (-2) = _____   (-8) + 9 = _____

(-6) + 6 = _____   (-7) + 3 = _____

(-1) + 3 = _____   5 + (-5) = _____

(-8) + (-2) = _____   (-4) + 4 = _____

(-9) + (-4) = _____   (-3) + 10 = _____

(-9) + (-1) = _____   (-3) + (-9) = _____

(-2) + (-3) = _____   (-2) + 3 = _____

Addition of Integers

Directions: Find the sum.

(-3) + 3 = _____   4 + (-1) = _____

4 + (-5) = _____   (-8) + (-8) = _____

6 + (-1) = _____   (-5) + (-9) = _____

1 + (-4) = _____   6 + (-3) = _____

4 + (-9) = _____   (-2) + (-2) = _____

(-4) + 1 = _____   (-4) + (-6) = _____

(-7) + (-9) = _____   4 + (-6) = _____

Decimals to Fractions

Directions: Convert to fractions and simplify if possible.

0.16 = _____

0.94 = _____

0.13 = _____

0.1 = _____

0.25 = _____

0.14 = _____

0.64 = _____

0.12 = _____

0.36 = _____

0.5 = _____

0.4 = _____

0.48 = _____

0.45 = _____

0.07 = _____

Decimals to Fractions

Directions: Convert to fractions and simplify if possible.

0.64 = _____   0.26 = _____

0.04 = _____   0.5 = _____

0.4 = _____   0.2 = _____

0.9 = _____   0.8 = _____

0.75 = _____   0.72 = _____

0.73 = _____   0.74 = _____

0.08 = _____   0.24 = _____

Decimals to Fractions

Directions: Convert to fractions and simplify if possible.

0.4 = _____

0.5 = _____

0.34 = _____

0.7 = _____

0.85 = _____

0.51 = _____

0.9 = _____

0.23 = _____

0.28 = _____

0.6 = _____

0.75 = _____

0.04 = _____

0.92 = _____

0.25 = _____

Decimals to Fractions

Directions: Convert to fractions and simplify if possible.

0.25 = _____	0.8 = _____
0.32 = _____	0.75 = _____
0.84 = _____	0.5 = _____
0.4 = _____	0.08 = _____
0.66 = _____	0.12 = _____
0.24 = _____	0.26 = _____
0.2 = _____	0.37 = _____

Decimals to Fractions

Directions: Convert to fractions and simplify if possible.

0.75 = _____   0.86 = _____

0.5 = _____   0.28 = _____

0.8 = _____   0.4 = _____

0.57 = _____   0.72 = _____

0.6 = _____   0.24 = _____

0.98 = _____   0.45 = _____

0.88 = _____   0.89 = _____

Subtraction of Integers

Directions: Find the difference.

$(-24) - (-6) =$ _____

$(-22) - (-7) =$ _____

$(-20) - (-22) =$ _____

$24 - (-14) =$ _____

$5 - (-6) =$ _____

$(-5) - 27 =$ _____

$(-13) - (-7) =$ _____

$1 - 5 =$ _____

$(-8) - (-4) =$ _____

$8 - 20 =$ _____

$(-10) - 6 =$ _____

$(-4) - 7 =$ _____

$(-18) - (-8) =$ _____

$(-22) - (-28) =$ _____

Subtraction of Integers

Directions: Find the difference.

8 – (-18) = _____

6 – (-7) = _____

26 – (-22) = _____

11 – (-13) = _____

24 – (-3) = _____

(-2) – 5 = _____

(-9) – 12 = _____

6 – (-5) = _____

(-3) – 1 = _____

(-26) – (-5) = _____

4 – (-6) = _____

(-12) – 7 = _____

(-3) – (-4) = _____

(-8) – (-28) = _____

Subtraction of Integers

Directions: Find the difference.

1 – (-5) = _____

3 – 12 = _____

(-8) – 21 = _____

1 – (-20) = _____

(-2) – 22 = _____

1 – (-23) = _____

15 – (-3) = _____

21 – (-11) = _____

14 – (-2) = _____

(-15) – 2 = _____

25 – (-17) = _____

(-26) – 12 = _____

4 – 27 = _____

8 – (-4) = _____

Subtraction of Integers

Directions: Find the difference.

$(-16) - (-4) =$ _____

$(-21) - 1 =$ _____

$(-13) - (-2) =$ _____

$1 - 3 =$ _____

$(-12) - 7 =$ _____

$1 - (-11) =$ _____

$(-23) - (-6) =$ _____

$1 - (-5) =$ _____

$8 - 12 =$ _____

$(-2) - 3 =$ _____

$8 - (-18) =$ _____

$(-19) - 2 =$ _____

$9 - (-3) =$ _____

$(-17) - (-24) =$ _____

Subtraction of Integers

Directions: Find the difference.

(-4) – (-3) = _____   7 – (-13) = _____

(-20) – (-4) = _____   (-5) – 30 = _____

22 – 27 = _____   (-9) – (-6) = _____

(-7) – (-5) = _____   (-18) – 14 = _____

(-3) – 8 = _____   28 – (-2) = _____

5 – (-5) = _____   15 – (-24) = _____

2 – (-9) = _____   (-5) – (-4) = _____

Division of Integers

Directions: Find the answer.

$77 \div (-7) =$ _____

$(-72) \div 12 =$ _____

$(-77) \div 11 =$ _____

$(-44) \div 11 =$ _____

$(-60) \div (-10) =$ _____

$84 \div (-3) =$ _____

$(-184) \div (-4) =$ _____

$(-72) \div (-6) =$ _____

$(-670) \div 10 =$ _____

$104 \div (-8) =$ _____

$(-44) \div (-11) =$ _____

$52 \div (-2) =$ _____

$(-116) \div 1 =$ _____

$110 \div (-10) =$ _____

Division of Integers

Directions: Find the answer.

$(-3) \div 3 =$ _____

$(-8) \div 8 =$ _____

$(-66) \div (-11) =$ _____

$(-36) \div 12 =$ _____

$55 \div (-5) =$ _____

$(-108) \div (-12) =$ _____

$(-177) \div 3 =$ _____

$(-104) \div (-4) =$ _____

$24 \div (-12) =$ _____

$110 \div (-11) =$ _____

$96 \div (-8) =$ _____

$66 \div (-11) =$ _____

$170 \div (-10) =$ _____

$(-110) \div (-11) =$ _____

Division of Integers

Directions: Find the answer.

$130 \div (-10) =$ _____

$16 \div (-4) =$ _____

$(-3) \div (-3) =$ _____

$(-114) \div (-2) =$ _____

$142 \div (-2) =$ _____

$(-180) \div (-4) =$ _____

$(-99) \div 3 =$ _____

$10 \div (-10) =$ _____

$(-160) \div (-4) =$ _____

$(-120) \div (-4) =$ _____

$33 \div (-11) =$ _____

$(-161) \div (-7) =$ _____

$120 \div (-12) =$ _____

$(-90) \div (-9) =$ _____

Division of Integers

Directions: Find the answer.

$(-144) \div (-12) =$ _____

$(-33) \div (-11) =$ _____

$(-48) \div 12 =$ _____

$(-72) \div (-9) =$ _____

$(-96) \div (-6) =$ _____

$30 \div (-10) =$ _____

$(-50) \div 10 =$ _____

$90 \div (-9) =$ _____

$11 \div (-11) =$ _____

$(-100) \div 10 =$ _____

$77 \div (-11) =$ _____

$187 \div (-11) =$ _____

$(-51) \div 1 =$ _____

$168 \div (-12) =$ _____

Division of Integers

Directions: Find the answer.

$(-57) \div 1 =$ _____

$(-77) \div 11 =$ _____

$96 \div (-4) =$ _____

$(-6) \div 3 =$ _____

$(-108) \div 3 =$ _____

$(-148) \div 4 =$ _____

$(-90) \div 10 =$ _____

$(-60) \div 2 =$ _____

$180 \div (-10) =$ _____

$(-156) \div (-12) =$ _____

$(-144) \div (-12) =$ _____

$(-121) \div (-11) =$ _____

$48 \div (-24) =$ _____

$240 \div (-12) =$ _____

Adding Fractions

1) $\frac{1}{2} + \frac{1}{2} =$

2) $\frac{1}{3} + \frac{3}{4} =$

3) $\frac{4}{5} + \frac{1}{2} =$

4) $\frac{1}{4} + \frac{1}{2} =$

5) $\frac{1}{4} + \frac{2}{3} =$

6) $\frac{1}{2} + \frac{2}{5} =$

7) $\frac{2}{3} + \frac{1}{3} =$

8) $\frac{1}{2} + \frac{1}{3} =$

9) $\frac{2}{3} + \frac{3}{5} =$

10) $\frac{3}{4} + \frac{1}{5} =$

11) $\frac{2}{3} + \frac{1}{5} =$

12) $\frac{1}{3} + \frac{1}{2} =$

13) $\frac{4}{5} + \frac{1}{5} =$

11/42

14) $\frac{1}{5} + \frac{2}{3} =$

15) $\frac{1}{2} + \frac{4}{5} =$

16) $\frac{3}{4} + \frac{1}{3} =$

17) $\frac{2}{5} + \frac{2}{3} =$

18) $\frac{1}{2} + \frac{1}{2} =$

19) $\frac{1}{2} + \frac{2}{3} =$

20) $\frac{1}{3} + \frac{1}{2} =$

21) $\frac{1}{2} + \frac{2}{3} =$

22) $\frac{1}{3} + \frac{1}{2} =$

23) $\frac{1}{2} + \frac{1}{2} =$

$\frac{1}{3}$

24) $\frac{1}{5} + 1 =$

25) $\frac{2}{3} + \frac{3}{4} =$

26) $\frac{1}{2} + \frac{1}{4} =$

27) $\frac{2}{3} + \frac{3}{5} =$

28) $\frac{1}{3} + \frac{1}{2} =$

29) $\frac{1}{5} + 1 =$

30) $\frac{1}{3} + \frac{1}{2} =$

1) $\frac{3}{5} + \frac{1}{2} =$

2) $\frac{1}{2} + \frac{2}{5} =$

3) $\frac{3}{5} + \frac{4}{5} =$

4) $\frac{1}{4} + \frac{3}{5} =$

5) $\frac{1}{3} + \frac{1}{2} =$

6) $\frac{4}{5} + \frac{2}{3} =$

7) $\frac{1}{4} + \frac{2}{3} =$

8) $\frac{3}{5} + \frac{1}{2} =$

9) $\frac{1}{3} + \frac{1}{4} =$

10) $\frac{3}{4} + \frac{1}{5} =$

11) $\frac{3}{4} + \frac{2}{5} =$

12) $\frac{1}{4} + \frac{3}{5} =$

13) $\frac{1}{3} + \frac{2}{5} =$

14) $\frac{1}{4} + \frac{2}{3} =$

15) $\frac{2}{3} + \frac{1}{2} =$

16) $\frac{1}{2} + \frac{1}{2} =$

17) $\frac{2}{3} + \frac{1}{2} =$

12/42

18) $\frac{1}{2} + \frac{1}{4} =$

19) $\frac{1}{3} + \frac{4}{5} =$

20) $\frac{2}{3} + \frac{1}{2} =$

21) $\frac{1}{2} + \frac{1}{3} =$

22) $\frac{1}{3} + \frac{1}{3} =$

23) $\frac{3}{4} + \frac{1}{2} =$

24) $\frac{2}{3} + \frac{1}{3} =$

25) $\frac{1}{2} + \frac{2}{3} =$

$\frac{1}{3}$

26) $\frac{3}{4} + \frac{3}{4} =$

27) $\frac{1}{2} + \frac{1}{2} =$

28) $\frac{2}{3} + \frac{1}{3} =$

29) $\frac{1}{3} + \frac{2}{5} =$

30) $\frac{1}{2} + \frac{3}{4} =$

1) $\frac{3}{5} + \frac{1}{3} =$

2) $\frac{3}{4} + \frac{2}{5} =$

3) $\frac{3}{5} + \frac{1}{3} =$

4) $\frac{1}{2} + \frac{1}{5} =$

5) $\frac{1}{3} + \frac{1}{2} =$

6) $\frac{1}{2} + \frac{1}{4} =$

7) $\frac{2}{3} + \frac{4}{5} =$

8) $\frac{3}{4} + \frac{1}{2} =$

9) $\frac{3}{4} + \frac{3}{4} =$

10) $\frac{1}{2} + \frac{1}{2} =$

11) $\frac{1}{4} + \frac{1}{2} =$

12) $\frac{2}{5} + \frac{1}{2} =$

13) $\frac{1}{4} + \frac{2}{5} =$

14) $\frac{1}{2} + \frac{3}{4} =$

15) $\frac{3}{4} + \frac{1}{5} =$

16) $\frac{1}{3} + \frac{3}{4} =$

17) $\frac{1}{4} + \frac{1}{2} =$

18) $\frac{2}{3} + \frac{2}{3} =$

19) $\frac{1}{3} + \frac{4}{5} =$

20) $\frac{1}{2} + \frac{1}{2} =$

21) $\frac{3}{4} + \frac{1}{2} =$

22) $\frac{4}{5} + \frac{1}{2} =$

23) $\frac{2}{3} + \frac{2}{3} =$

24) $\frac{1}{2} + \frac{3}{4} =$

25) $\frac{1}{4} + \frac{1}{3} =$

26) $\frac{1}{2} + \frac{2}{5} =$

27) $\frac{2}{3} + \frac{1}{2} =$

28) $\frac{3}{5} + \frac{1}{2} =$

29) $\frac{2}{3} + \frac{1}{2} =$

30) $\frac{3}{5} + \frac{2}{3} =$

13/42

⅓

1) $\frac{3}{4} + \frac{2}{3} =$ 2) $\frac{1}{2} + \frac{1}{2} =$

3) $\frac{1}{4} + \frac{1}{3} =$ 4) $\frac{1}{5} + \frac{1}{3} =$

5) $\frac{1}{2} + \frac{3}{4} =$ 6) $\frac{1}{2} + \frac{1}{3} =$

7) $\frac{1}{3} + \frac{1}{2} =$ 8) $\frac{1}{3} + \frac{2}{3} =$

9) $\frac{3}{4} + \frac{3}{4} =$ 10) $\frac{2}{5} + \frac{2}{3} =$

11) $\frac{2}{3} + \frac{3}{4} =$ 12) $\frac{1}{2} + \frac{3}{5} =$

13) $\frac{1}{2} + \frac{1}{2} =$ 14) $\frac{4}{5} + \frac{1}{3} =$

15) $\frac{1}{2} + \frac{2}{3} =$ 16) $\frac{2}{3} + \frac{1}{2} =$

17) $\frac{1}{2} + \frac{1}{3} =$ 14/42 18) $\frac{2}{5} + \frac{1}{5} =$

19) $\frac{1}{3} + \frac{1}{2} =$ 20) $\frac{1}{3} + \frac{3}{5} =$

21) $\frac{1}{2} + \frac{1}{2} =$ 22) $\frac{1}{3} + \frac{3}{4} =$

23) $\frac{1}{2} + \frac{1}{2} =$ 24) $\frac{1}{4} + \frac{2}{3} =$

25) $\frac{1}{2} + \frac{1}{3} =$ 26) $\frac{1}{2} + \frac{2}{3} =$

27) $\frac{4}{5} + \frac{1}{2} =$ 1/3 28) $\frac{2}{5} + \frac{1}{2} =$

29) $\frac{4}{5} + \frac{2}{3} =$ 30) $\frac{1}{2} + \frac{1}{4} =$

1) $\frac{1}{3} + \frac{1}{3} =$

2) $\frac{2}{5} + \frac{3}{4} =$

3) $\frac{2}{3} + \frac{3}{5} =$

4) $\frac{2}{3} + \frac{1}{2} =$

5) $\frac{2}{5} + \frac{1}{2} =$

6) $\frac{2}{3} + 1 =$

7) $\frac{1}{5} + \frac{1}{3} =$

8) $\frac{4}{5} + \frac{1}{2} =$

9) $\frac{2}{5} + \frac{3}{4} =$

10) $\frac{1}{2} + \frac{1}{2} =$

11) $\frac{1}{2} + \frac{3}{5} =$

12) $\frac{1}{4} + \frac{1}{4} =$

13) $\frac{1}{2} + \frac{1}{2} =$

14) $\frac{1}{2} + \frac{4}{5} =$

15) $\frac{1}{3} + \frac{1}{2} =$

16) $\frac{1}{2} + \frac{1}{4} =$

17) $\frac{1}{3} + \frac{1}{3} =$

18) $\frac{4}{5} + \frac{3}{4} =$

19) $\frac{1}{2} + \frac{1}{2} =$

20) $\frac{2}{3} + \frac{3}{4} =$

21) $\frac{1}{3} + \frac{4}{5} =$

22) $\frac{1}{2} + \frac{2}{3} =$

23) $\frac{1}{2} + \frac{1}{3} =$

24) $\frac{2}{3} + \frac{2}{3} =$

25) $\frac{3}{4} + \frac{2}{5} =$

26) $1 + \frac{3}{5} =$

27) $\frac{1}{2} + \frac{1}{5} =$

28) $\frac{2}{5} + \frac{1}{2} =$

29) $\frac{1}{2} + \frac{4}{5} =$

30) $\frac{4}{5} + \frac{1}{2} =$

15/42

1/3

1) $\frac{7}{2} + \frac{33}{8} =$

2) $\frac{19}{8} + \frac{7}{2} =$

3) $4 + \frac{7}{4} =$

4) $\frac{9}{2} + \frac{2}{5} =$

5) $\frac{15}{7} + \frac{5}{3} =$

6) $\frac{17}{5} + \frac{4}{5} =$

7) $\frac{39}{8} + \frac{19}{5} =$

8) $5 + \frac{19}{4} =$

9) $\frac{17}{5} + \frac{1}{2} =$

10) $3 + \frac{9}{8} =$

11) $\frac{9}{4} + \frac{9}{4} =$

12) $\frac{5}{2} + \frac{1}{3} =$

13) $\frac{5}{2} + \frac{7}{3} =$

14) $\frac{7}{5} + 3 =$

15) $\frac{11}{6} + \frac{31}{8} =$

16) $\frac{35}{8} + \frac{2}{3} =$

16/42

17) $\frac{9}{2} + \frac{17}{8} =$

18) $\frac{3}{7} + \frac{3}{2} =$

19) $\frac{4}{3} + \frac{10}{3} =$

20) $\frac{7}{3} + \frac{11}{5} =$

21) $3 + \frac{3}{7} =$

22) $\frac{12}{7} + \frac{6}{5} =$

23) $\frac{3}{8} + \frac{12}{7} =$

24) $1 + \frac{4}{3} =$

25) $4 + \frac{13}{4} =$

26) $\frac{29}{8} + \frac{9}{2} =$

$\frac{1}{3}$

27) $\frac{9}{8} + \frac{21}{5} =$

28) $\frac{17}{6} + 5 =$

29) $3 + \frac{15}{7} =$

30) $\frac{7}{3} + \frac{7}{2} =$

1) $\frac{1}{8} + \frac{31}{7} =$

2) $\frac{11}{3} + \frac{9}{2} =$

3) $\frac{10}{7} + 3 =$

4) $\frac{7}{2} + 4 =$

5) $\frac{1}{7} + 1 =$

6) $\frac{7}{3} + \frac{4}{3} =$

7) $\frac{23}{5} + \frac{13}{5} =$

8) $\frac{17}{4} + \frac{19}{4} =$

9) $\frac{5}{8} + \frac{7}{8} =$

10) $\frac{5}{2} + \frac{13}{5} =$

11) $5 + \frac{11}{8} =$

12) $\frac{19}{5} + \frac{7}{2} =$

13) $\frac{19}{6} + \frac{1}{3} =$

14) $\frac{12}{7} + \frac{20}{7} =$

15) $\frac{20}{7} + \frac{17}{8} =$

16) $\frac{19}{4} + 2 =$

17) $\frac{9}{2} + \frac{16}{3} =$

18) $\frac{17}{7} + \frac{11}{5} =$

19) $\frac{3}{5} + \frac{17}{4} =$

20) $\frac{4}{3} + \frac{8}{7} =$

21) $\frac{2}{3} + \frac{13}{4} =$

22) $\frac{7}{2} + \frac{22}{7} =$

23) $\frac{5}{2} + \frac{9}{2} =$

24) $\frac{29}{7} + 3 =$

25) $\frac{13}{4} + \frac{1}{6} =$

26) $\frac{4}{5} + \frac{14}{5} =$

27) $\frac{12}{5} + \frac{23}{7} =$

28) $\frac{2}{5} + \frac{3}{4} =$

29) $\frac{22}{7} + 3 =$

30) $\frac{23}{7} + \frac{30}{7} =$

17/42

1/3

1) $\frac{1}{6} + \frac{39}{8} =$

2) $\frac{14}{3} + \frac{5}{2} =$

3) $\frac{5}{8} + \frac{3}{5} =$

4) $5 + \frac{7}{2} =$

5) $\frac{5}{8} + 5 =$

6) $\frac{6}{5} + 4 =$

7) $\frac{8}{7} + \frac{15}{4} =$

8) $\frac{37}{8} + 5 =$

9) $3 + \frac{4}{3} =$

10) $4 + \frac{1}{3} =$

11) $\frac{1}{3} + \frac{5}{2} =$

12) $2 + \frac{13}{4} =$

13) $\frac{9}{4} + \frac{5}{7} =$

14) $1 + \frac{3}{4} =$

15) $\frac{34}{7} + \frac{21}{5} =$

16) $\frac{3}{2} + \frac{7}{2} =$

17) $\frac{31}{8} + \frac{11}{6} =$

18) $\frac{24}{5} + \frac{5}{2} =$

18/42

19) $\frac{9}{8} + \frac{3}{7} =$

20) $\frac{5}{2} + \frac{14}{3} =$

21) $\frac{7}{3} + 5 =$

22) $\frac{5}{3} + 3 =$

23) $2 + \frac{2}{3} =$

24) $\frac{1}{2} + 4 =$

25) $\frac{1}{3} + \frac{3}{2} =$

26) $4 + \frac{25}{7} =$

$\frac{1}{3}$

27) $4 + \frac{19}{4} =$

28) $\frac{7}{2} + \frac{15}{4} =$

29) $\frac{16}{7} + 3 =$

30) $\frac{4}{7} + \frac{24}{5} =$

1) $\frac{7}{2} + \frac{5}{4} =$

2) $5 + \frac{22}{5} =$

3) $\frac{5}{2} + \frac{6}{5} =$

4) $\frac{3}{2} + \frac{1}{2} =$

5) $\frac{35}{8} + \frac{3}{4} =$

6) $\frac{9}{4} + 5 =$

7) $3 + \frac{30}{7} =$

8) $4 + \frac{1}{2} =$

9) $\frac{1}{7} + 2 =$

10) $\frac{11}{5} + \frac{10}{3} =$

11) $\frac{16}{7} + \frac{9}{2} =$

12) $\frac{3}{2} + \frac{9}{2} =$

13) $5 + \frac{4}{5} =$

14) $\frac{25}{8} + \frac{23}{7} =$

15) $\frac{21}{8} + \frac{9}{2} =$

16) $5 + \frac{5}{6} =$

17) $\frac{3}{2} + \frac{3}{5} =$

18) $\frac{16}{5} + \frac{5}{3} =$

19) $\frac{16}{5} + 1 =$

20) $\frac{5}{3} + \frac{1}{2} =$

21) $\frac{32}{7} + 2 =$

22) $\frac{21}{5} + 3 =$

23) $\frac{3}{2} + \frac{19}{4} =$

24) $\frac{10}{3} + 3 =$

25) $\frac{9}{2} + 4 =$

26) $3 + \frac{9}{8} =$

27) $\frac{7}{2} + 1 =$

28) $5 + \frac{7}{2} =$

29) $\frac{15}{4} + \frac{1}{2} =$

30) $\frac{26}{7} + 2 =$

19/42

1/3

1) $\frac{17}{8} + 2 =$

2) $\frac{7}{2} + \frac{11}{8} =$

3) $\frac{3}{2} + \frac{7}{2} =$

4) $\frac{8}{3} + \frac{1}{3} =$

5) $5 + \frac{4}{3} =$

6) $\frac{23}{8} + \frac{3}{2} =$

7) $\frac{19}{4} + \frac{21}{5} =$

8) $\frac{5}{3} + \frac{5}{2} =$

9) $\frac{1}{8} + \frac{13}{5} =$

10) $5 + \frac{1}{2} =$

11) $\frac{22}{7} + \frac{6}{7} =$

12) $\frac{5}{4} + 2 =$

13) $\frac{2}{3} + \frac{7}{4} =$

14) $\frac{7}{3} + 4 =$

15) $\frac{7}{2} + \frac{9}{5} =$

16) $\frac{7}{2} + \frac{21}{5} =$

17) $\frac{5}{2} + 3 =$

18) $\frac{15}{7} + \frac{3}{2} =$

19) $\frac{29}{7} + \frac{29}{7} =$

20/42

20) $\frac{30}{7} + 5 =$

21) $\frac{4}{7} + 1 =$

22) $\frac{1}{6} + \frac{30}{7} =$

23) $\frac{33}{7} + \frac{9}{7} =$

24) $\frac{18}{5} + \frac{35}{8} =$

25) $\frac{9}{7} + \frac{8}{3} =$

26) $\frac{12}{5} + \frac{7}{3} =$

27) $\frac{5}{6} + \frac{1}{4} =$

28) $5 + \frac{15}{4} =$

29) $5 + \frac{11}{4} =$

30) $3 + \frac{19}{5} =$

Addition of Integers

Directions: Find the sum.

(-8) + (-7) = _____   (-25) + (-5) = _____

(-9) + (-1) = _____   (-4) + (-30) = _____

(-9) + (-2) = _____   4 + (-7) = _____

(-3) + (-19) = _____   (-6) + 6 = _____

(-3) + (-5) = _____   (-3) + 12 = _____

(-4) + 9 = _____   (-22) + (-28) = _____

(-13) + 25 = _____   (-5) + (-29) = _____

Addition of Integers

Directions: Find the sum.

12 + (-4) = _____

6 + (-8) = _____

10 + (-3) = _____

16 + (-2) = _____

(-16) + 28 = _____

15 + (-4) = _____

(-21) + 1 = _____

(-27) + 29 = _____

4 + (-5) = _____

6 + (-7) = _____

16 + (-22) = _____

22 + (-4) = _____

(-30) + 14 = _____

(-4) + 6 = _____

Addition of Integers

Directions: Find the sum.

14 + (-7) = _____

(-24) + (-21) = _____

4 + (-16) = _____

(-9) + (-2) = _____

27 + (-4) = _____

(-16) + 6 = _____

(-30) + (-14) = _____

(-9) + 22 = _____

(-1) + 4 = _____

(-16) + 1 = _____

(-12) + 4 = _____

(-3) + (-5) = _____

9 + (-23) = _____

11 + (-14) = _____

Name: _____   Date: _____

Addition of Integers

Directions: Find the sum.

(-7) + 7 = _____

(-29) + (-7) = _____

(-5) + 5 = _____

4 + (-8) = _____

18 + (-1) = _____

(-20) + 2 = _____

(-1) + 21 = _____

24 + (-8) = _____

(-20) + 22 = _____

(-7) + 1 = _____

1 + (-5) = _____

(-6) + 3 = _____

(-8) + 2 = _____

(-18) + (-3) = _____

Addition of Integers

Directions: Find the sum.

(-4) + (-8) = _____

(-6) + 20 = _____

17 + (-12) = _____

(-2) + 6 = _____

(-24) + (-25) = _____

(-2) + 25 = _____

15 + (-5) = _____

(-18) + (-27) = _____

3 + (-28) = _____

(-14) + 3 = _____

(-16) + (-28) = _____

(-2) + 6 = _____

9 + (-2) = _____

4 + (-2) = _____

Add & Subtract

Directions: Find the solution.

2 + 24 + 40 + 39 − (33 − 30) =

_____

2 + 24 + 40 + 39 − 33 − 30 =

_____

(34 − 24) + (3 + 39) − (3 + 38) =

_____

36 + 39 − (34 − 12) − 20 + 9 =

_____

(17 + 8 + 26 − 15 − 5) + 10 =

_____

38 − 6 + 17 + 29 − (36 + 10) =

_____

39 − (15 − 14) + (40 − 38 − 1) =

_____

Add & Subtract

Directions: Find the solution.

$(26 + 14) - (15 + 15) - (3 + 7) =$

_____

$44 - (54 - 20 - 10 - 5 - 5) =$

_____

$24 + 29 - (24 - 17 + 4) + 10 =$

_____

$39 + 27 + 4 - 31 - (18 - 12) =$

_____

$35 + (36 - 25 + 27) - 30 - 13 =$

_____

$50 + (50 - 20) - (39 - 27 - 10) =$

_____

$50 + 50 - 20 - 39 - 27 - 10 =$

_____

Add & Subtract

Directions: Find the solution.

$(26 + 17) + (12 + 21) + (35 + 18) =$

_____

$26 + 17 + 12 + 21 + 35 + 18 =$

_____

$(26 + 17) - (12 + 21) + (35 + 18) =$

_____

$26 + 17 - 12 + 21 + 35 + 18 =$

_____

$24 - (3 + 9) + (28 + 40 + 40) =$

_____

$36 - (3 + 5 - 4 - 3) + 4 =$

_____

$65 + 27 + 33 - (33 + 27 + 65) =$

_____

Add & Subtract

Directions: Find the solution.

12 + 8 + 16 - (12 + 8 - 16) =

_____

36 - (1 + 2 + 3 - 2 - 1) =

_____

36 - (1 + 2 + 3 - 2) - 1 =

_____

10 + 31 + 40 - (31 + 6 - 9) =

_____

25 + 11 + 4 + 30 - (19 + 27) =

_____

1 + 6 + 38 + 30 + (13 + 13) =

_____

1 + 6 + 38 + 30 - (13 + 13) =

_____

Add & Subtract

Directions: Find the solution.

(29 – 14 + 33) – (29 – 14 + 33) =

_____

(29 – 14 + 33) – (29 – 14) + 33 =

_____

(29 – 14 + 33) – (29 – 14) – 33 =

_____

16 + 28 + (23 + 35) – (16 + 28) =

_____

33 + 11 + 14 + 2 – (21 + 33) =

_____

54 – (37 + 15) – (37 + 14) – 1 =

_____

50 + 10 – (10 + 5) – 5 – 20 =

_____

Prime Factor Trees

Complete the factor trees to find the prime factors of each number.

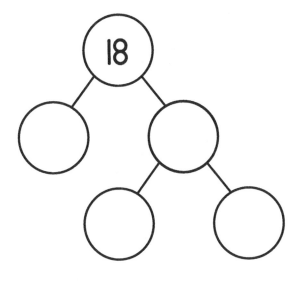

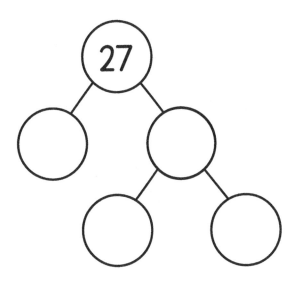

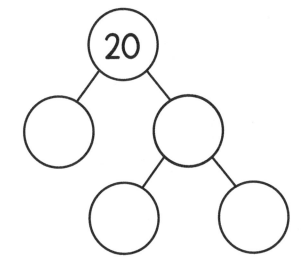

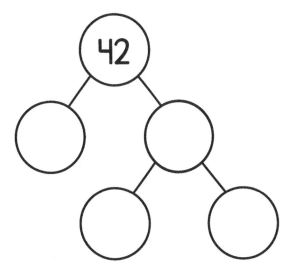

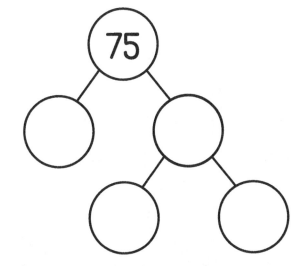

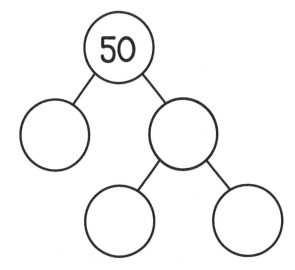

Prime Factor Trees

Complete the factor trees to find the prime factors of each number.

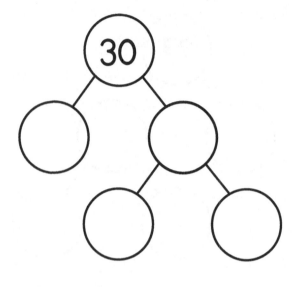

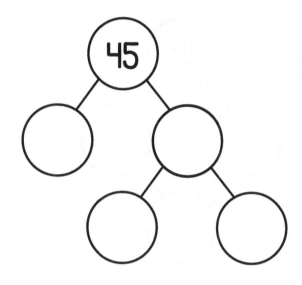

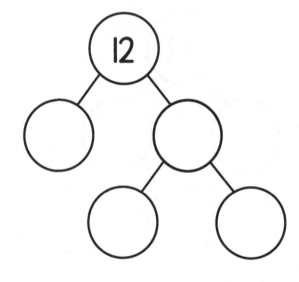

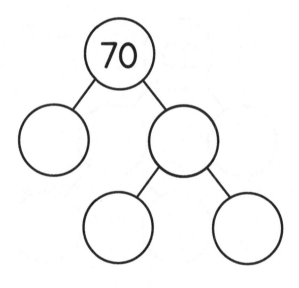

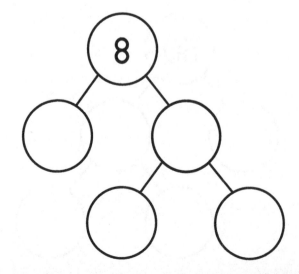

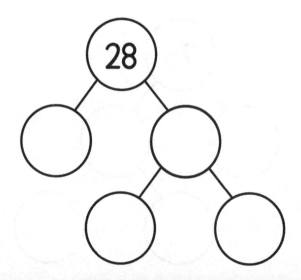

Prime Factor Trees

Complete the factor trees to find the prime factors of each number.

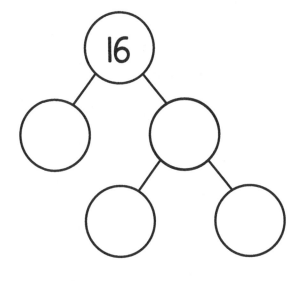

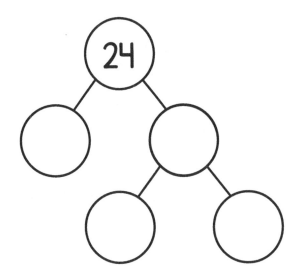

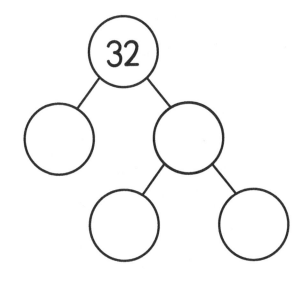

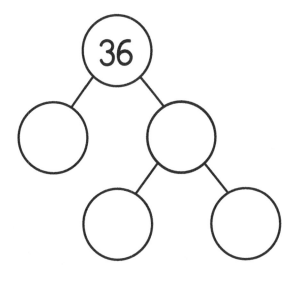

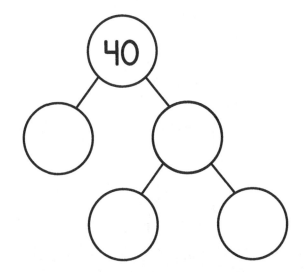

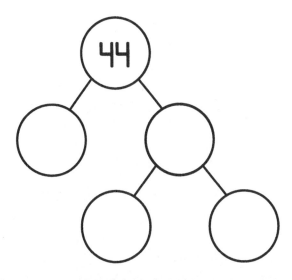

Prime Factor Trees

Complete the factor trees to find the prime factors of each number.

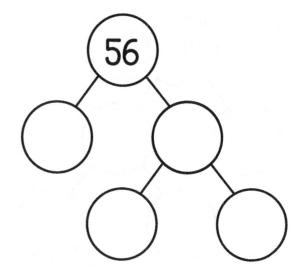

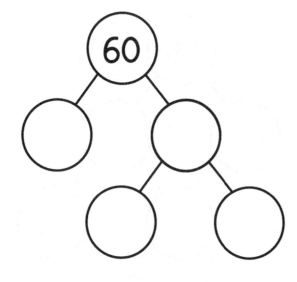

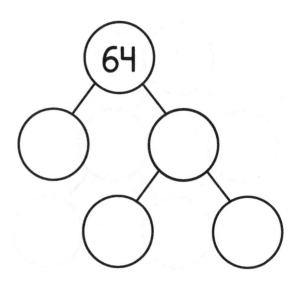

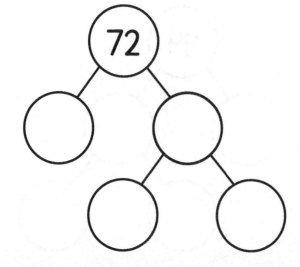

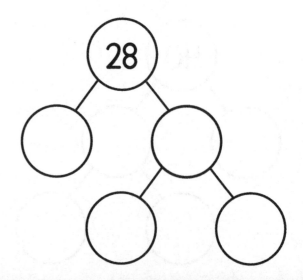

Prime Factor Trees

Complete the factor trees to find the prime factors of each number.

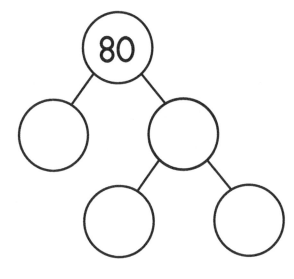

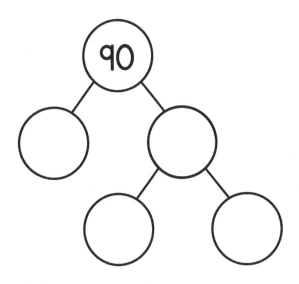

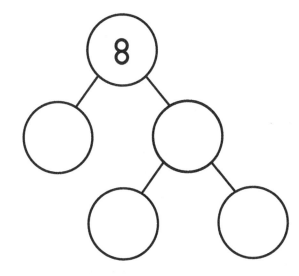

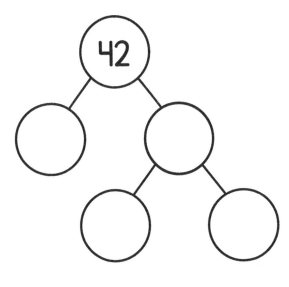

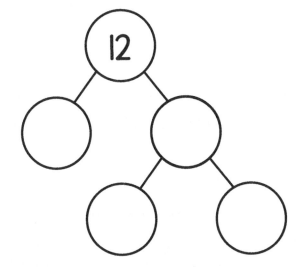

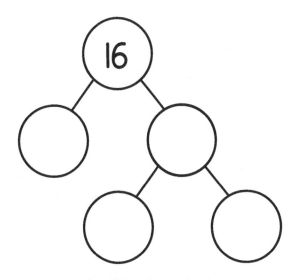

Add & Subtract

Directions: Find the solution.

20 − (12 − 7) = _____

(18 − 16) + 12 = _____

13 − (20 − 9) = _____

16 − (19 − 3) = _____

(19 − 17) + 7 = _____

(18 − 11) + 13 = _____

12 − (6 + 6) = _____

Add & Subtract

Directions: Find the solution.

13 – (4 + 9) = _____

1 + (12 – 2) = _____

(16 – 2) – 12 = _____

15 – (17 – 3) = _____

16 – (11 – 2) = _____

11 + (19 – 1) = _____

(15 – 1) – 10 = _____

Add & Subtract

Directions: Find the solution.

15 − (11 − 8) = _____

11 + (8 − 1) = _____

20 − (4 + 14) = _____

(19 − 10) − 7 = _____

18 − (13 − 5) = _____

13 − (10 − 7) = _____

17 − (9 + 4) = _____

Name: _____   Date: _____

Add & Subtract

Directions: Find the solution.

$(11 - 4) - 3 =$ _____

$14 - (17 - 5) =$ _____

$15 - (2 + 7) =$ _____

$14 + (11 - 8) =$ _____

$16 - (9 + 3) =$ _____

$17 - (11 + 5) =$ _____

$(18 - 6) + 2 =$ _____

Add & Subtract

Directions: Find the solution.

2 + (12 – 1) = _____

17 – (6 + 6) = _____

5 + (12 + 2) = _____

5 + (4 – 1) = _____

1 – (11 – 10) = _____

18 – (2 + 4) = _____

5 + (11 – 6) = _____

Multiplying fractions

Directions: Find the product.

$\dfrac{5}{7} \times \dfrac{2}{4} =$

$\dfrac{2}{5} \times \dfrac{1}{2} =$

$\dfrac{1}{2} \times \dfrac{2}{8} =$

$\dfrac{2}{6} \times \dfrac{1}{7} =$

$\dfrac{5}{10} \times \dfrac{8}{9} =$

$\dfrac{4}{5} \times \dfrac{2}{11} =$

$\dfrac{7}{8} \times \dfrac{2}{4} =$

Multiplying fractions

Directions: Find the product.

$$\frac{8}{12} \times \frac{4}{10} =$$

$$\frac{1}{2} \times \frac{1}{3} =$$

$$\frac{3}{4} \times \frac{1}{7} =$$

$$\frac{3}{8} \times \frac{2}{3} =$$

$$\frac{9}{10} \times \frac{9}{12} =$$

$$\frac{5}{7} \times \frac{1}{4} =$$

$$\frac{7}{9} \times \frac{1}{7} =$$

Multiplying fractions

Directions: Find the product.

$$\frac{3}{7} \times \frac{4}{8} =$$

$$\frac{2}{4} \times \frac{3}{12} =$$

$$\frac{4}{5} \times \frac{1}{4} =$$

$$\frac{3}{8} \times \frac{1}{9} =$$

$$\frac{2}{7} \times \frac{3}{5} =$$

$$\frac{4}{6} \times \frac{3}{10} =$$

$$\frac{4}{10} \times \frac{5}{8} =$$

Multiplying fractions

Directions: Find the product.

$$\frac{6}{10} \times \frac{1}{2} =$$

$$\frac{1}{5} \times \frac{4}{8} =$$

$$\frac{1}{2} \times \frac{6}{11} =$$

$$\frac{4}{6} \times \frac{5}{7} =$$

$$\frac{3}{8} \times \frac{2}{9} =$$

$$\frac{8}{10} \times \frac{1}{2} =$$

$$\frac{4}{9} \times \frac{7}{8} =$$

Multiplying fractions

Directions: Find the product.

$$\frac{4}{5} \times \frac{2}{3} =$$

$$\frac{1}{3} \times \frac{4}{6} =$$

$$\frac{1}{2} \times \frac{2}{11} =$$

$$\frac{4}{6} \times \frac{1}{2} =$$

$$\frac{5}{11} \times \frac{3}{9} =$$

$$\frac{1}{2} \times \frac{2}{3} =$$

$$\frac{4}{8} \times \frac{2}{7} =$$

Adding unlike fractions

Directions: Find the sum.

$\dfrac{5}{10} + \dfrac{6}{30} =$

$\dfrac{7}{8} + \dfrac{1}{2} =$

$\dfrac{1}{3} + \dfrac{3}{15} =$

$\dfrac{5}{6} + \dfrac{8}{10} =$

$\dfrac{19}{30} + \dfrac{32}{40} =$

$\dfrac{19}{20} + \dfrac{6}{30} =$

$\dfrac{7}{9} + \dfrac{5}{18} =$

Adding unlike fractions

Directions: Find the sum.

$$\frac{9}{15} + \frac{1}{3} =$$

$$\frac{3}{15} + \frac{1}{7} =$$

$$\frac{20}{50} + \frac{1}{6} =$$

$$\frac{2}{3} + \frac{22}{50} =$$

$$\frac{6}{9} + \frac{3}{4} =$$

$$\frac{5}{12} + \frac{17}{18} =$$

$$\frac{5}{11} + \frac{14}{25} =$$

Adding unlike fractions

Directions: Find the sum.

$$\frac{1}{14} + \frac{6}{18} =$$

$$\frac{5}{20} + \frac{6}{8} =$$

$$\frac{4}{11} + \frac{2}{3} =$$

$$\frac{70}{100} + \frac{2}{4} =$$

$$\frac{4}{25} + \frac{5}{30} =$$

$$\frac{1}{7} + \frac{3}{9} =$$

$$\frac{6}{10} + \frac{32}{40} =$$

Adding unlike fractions

Directions: Find the sum.

$\dfrac{2}{4} + \dfrac{14}{16} =$

$\dfrac{4}{8} + \dfrac{6}{11} =$

$\dfrac{3}{25} + \dfrac{7}{30} =$

$\dfrac{2}{20} + \dfrac{10}{18} =$

$\dfrac{48}{100} + \dfrac{12}{15} =$

$\dfrac{3}{9} + \dfrac{5}{6} =$

$\dfrac{28}{30} + \dfrac{1}{2} =$

Adding unlike fractions

Directions: Find the sum.

$$\frac{1}{10} + \frac{10}{40} =$$

$$\frac{23}{30} + \frac{4}{15} =$$

$$\frac{2}{3} + \frac{6}{10} =$$

$$\frac{14}{15} + \frac{8}{9} =$$

$$\frac{40}{50} + \frac{20}{30} =$$

$$\frac{2}{14} + \frac{3}{12} =$$

$$\frac{41}{100} + \frac{6}{7} =$$

Dividing fractions

Directions: Find the answer.

$$\frac{8}{9} \div \frac{2}{9} =$$

$$\frac{2}{3} \div \frac{1}{11} =$$

$$\frac{1}{5} \div \frac{2}{4} =$$

$$\frac{1}{8} \div \frac{2}{3} =$$

$$\frac{5}{10} \div \frac{7}{11} =$$

$$\frac{6}{11} \div \frac{1}{6} =$$

$$\frac{8}{9} \div \frac{6}{9} =$$

Dividing fractions

Directions: Find the answer.

$\dfrac{1}{7} \div \dfrac{2}{11} =$

$\dfrac{7}{10} \div \dfrac{5}{9} =$

$\dfrac{2}{4} \div \dfrac{1}{4} =$

$\dfrac{1}{5} \div \dfrac{1}{3} =$

$\dfrac{2}{10} \div \dfrac{9}{11} =$

$\dfrac{2}{12} \div \dfrac{2}{5} =$

$\dfrac{4}{11} \div \dfrac{4}{12} =$

Dividing fractions

Directions: Find the answer.

$$\frac{3}{7} \div \frac{1}{3} =$$

$$\frac{1}{8} \div \frac{4}{5} =$$

$$\frac{2}{11} \div \frac{5}{10} =$$

$$\frac{2}{8} \div \frac{1}{3} =$$

$$\frac{5}{7} \div \frac{2}{7} =$$

$$\frac{1}{3} \div \frac{7}{9} =$$

$$\frac{5}{10} \div \frac{3}{5} =$$

Dividing fractions

Directions: Find the answer.

$$\frac{2}{5} \div \frac{11}{12} =$$

$$\frac{1}{7} \div \frac{2}{4} =$$

$$\frac{5}{10} \div \frac{1}{3} =$$

$$\frac{7}{11} \div \frac{6}{10} =$$

$$\frac{2}{10} \div \frac{1}{5} =$$

$$\frac{3}{7} \div \frac{4}{8} =$$

$$\frac{5}{12} \div \frac{1}{4} =$$

Dividing fractions

Directions: Find the answer.

$\dfrac{2}{3} \div \dfrac{7}{10} =$

$\dfrac{3}{4} \div \dfrac{1}{4} =$

$\dfrac{3}{10} \div \dfrac{2}{4} =$

$\dfrac{9}{12} \div \dfrac{8}{9} =$

$\dfrac{7}{9} \div \dfrac{8}{10} =$

$\dfrac{3}{4} \div \dfrac{3}{6} =$

$\dfrac{2}{3} \div \dfrac{3}{12} =$

Made in the USA
Las Vegas, NV
12 February 2024

85708981R00059